OPOSSUMS

CURIOUS FOX BOOKS

© 2024 by Curious Fox Books™, an imprint of Fox Chapel Publishing Company, Inc., 903 Square Street, Mount Joy, PA 17552.

Kids' Backyard Safari: Opossums is a revision of *Backyard Jungle Safari: Opossums*, first published in 2015 by Purple Toad Publishing, Inc. Reproduction of its contents is strictly prohibited without written permission from the rights holder.

ISBN 979-8-89094-004-9

Library of Congress Control Number: 2023942298

ABOUT THE AUTHOR: Ann Tatlock is the author of ten novels. Her works have received numerous awards, including the Silver Angel Award from Excellence in Media and the Midwest Book Award. She lives in the Blue Ridge Mountains of Western North Carolina with her husband, daughter, three Chihuahuas and a guinea pig named Lilly.

To learn more about the other great books from Fox Chapel Publishing, or to find a retailer near you, call toll-free 800-457-9112 or visit us at *www.FoxChapelPublishing.com*.

We are always looking for talented authors. To submit an idea, please send a brief inquiry to acquisitions@foxchapelpublishing.com.

Fox Chapel Publishing makes every effort to use environmentally friendly paper for printing.

Printed in China
First Printing

OPOSSUMS

Explore Their World and Learn Fun Facts

Ann Tatlock

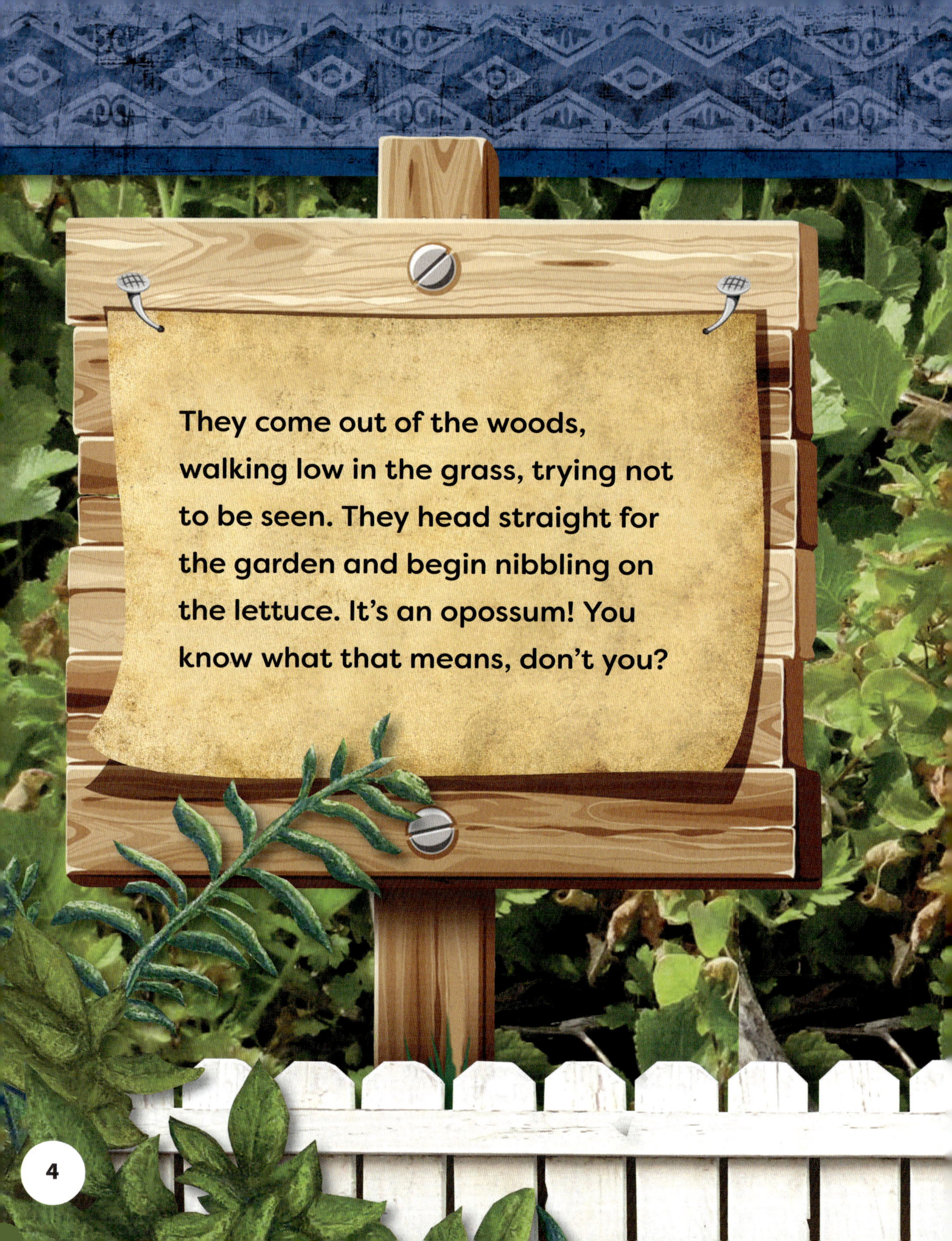

They come out of the woods, walking low in the grass, trying not to be seen. They head straight for the garden and begin nibbling on the lettuce. It's an opossum! You know what that means, don't you?

Opossums are nocturnal. They come out at night in search of food. Their eyes have large pupils so they can see in the dark.

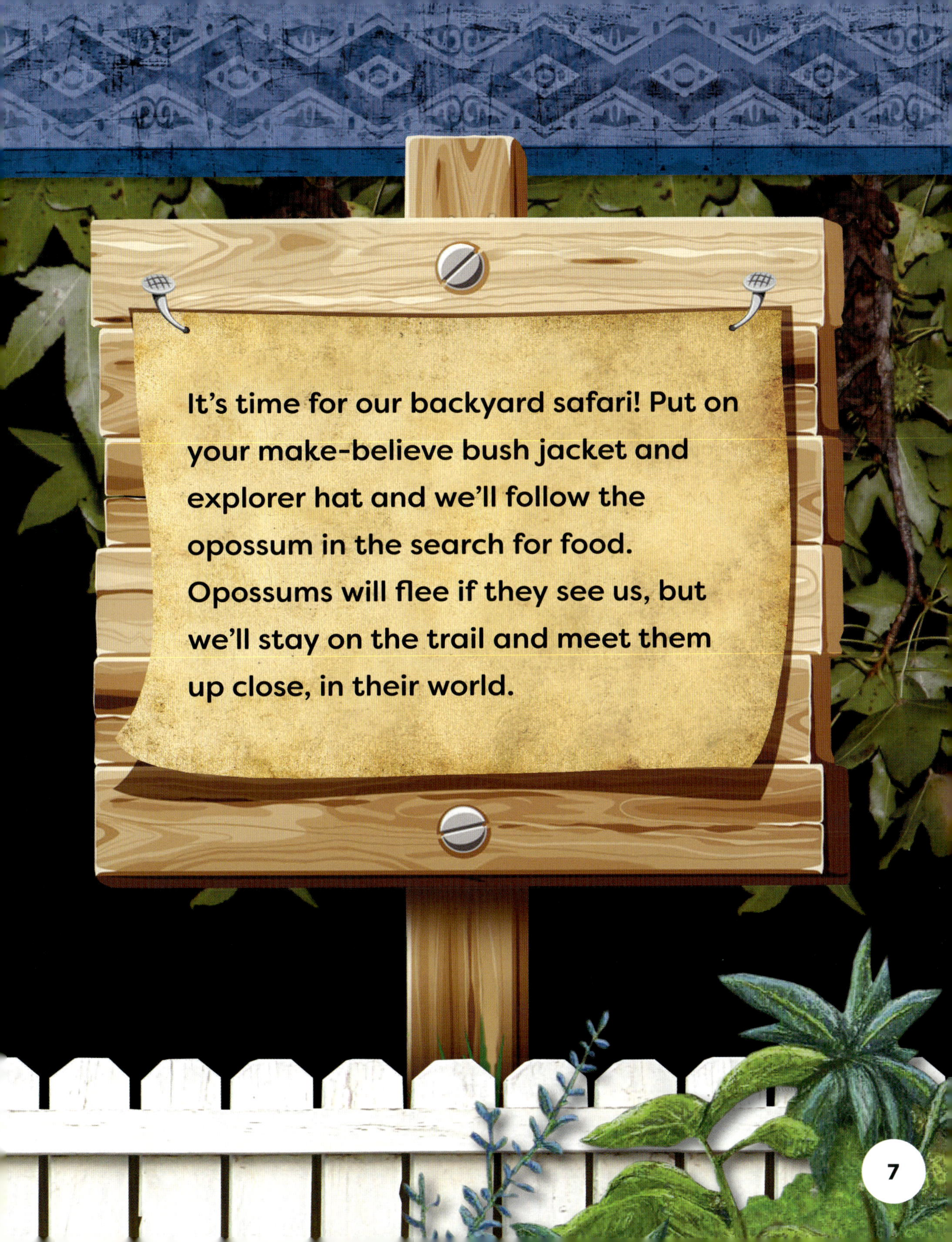
It's time for our backyard safari! Put on your make-believe bush jacket and explorer hat and we'll follow the opossum in the search for food. Opossums will flee if they see us, but we'll stay on the trail and meet them up close, in their world.

There are more than 90 species of opossums. The little creatures eating supper in our garden are Virginia opossums, the only kind found in North America.

The opossum lives as far south as Nicaragua and as far north as Canada. There are opossum "cousins" in Australasia, a region that includes Australia, Tasmania, and New Zealand.

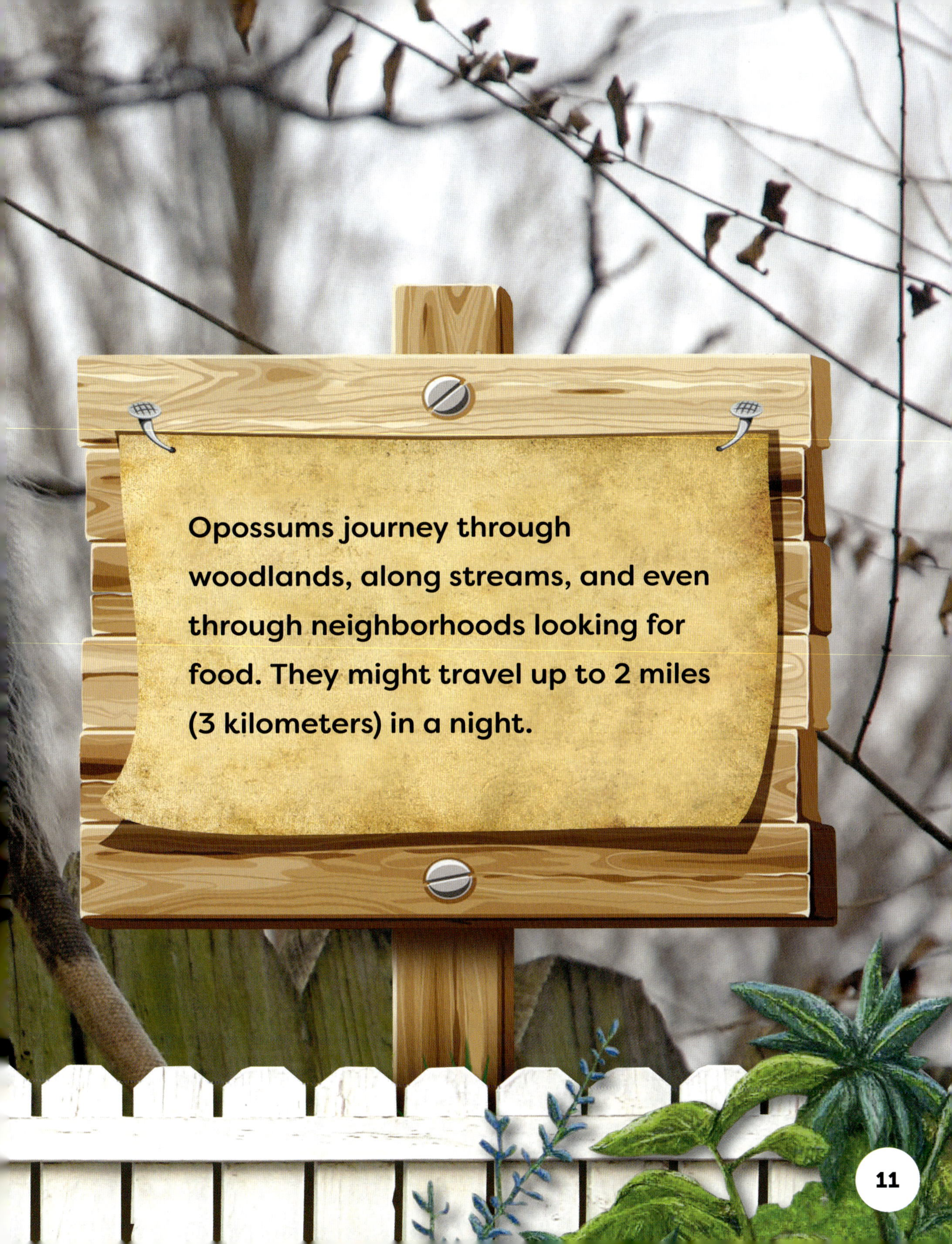
Opossums journey through woodlands, along streams, and even through neighborhoods looking for food. They might travel up to 2 miles (3 kilometers) in a night.

They are very quiet, "speaking" only when necessary. Opossums make clicking sounds when calling for a mate and growling, hissing, or squawking sounds when threatened by a predator.

Opossums scamper up into trees when they're frightened.

Opossums are afraid of us because humans are among their natural predators. Others include coyotes, foxes, bobcats, dogs, and hawks.

If an opossum isn't killed by a predator first, it can live for 2 to 4 years.
Coyote

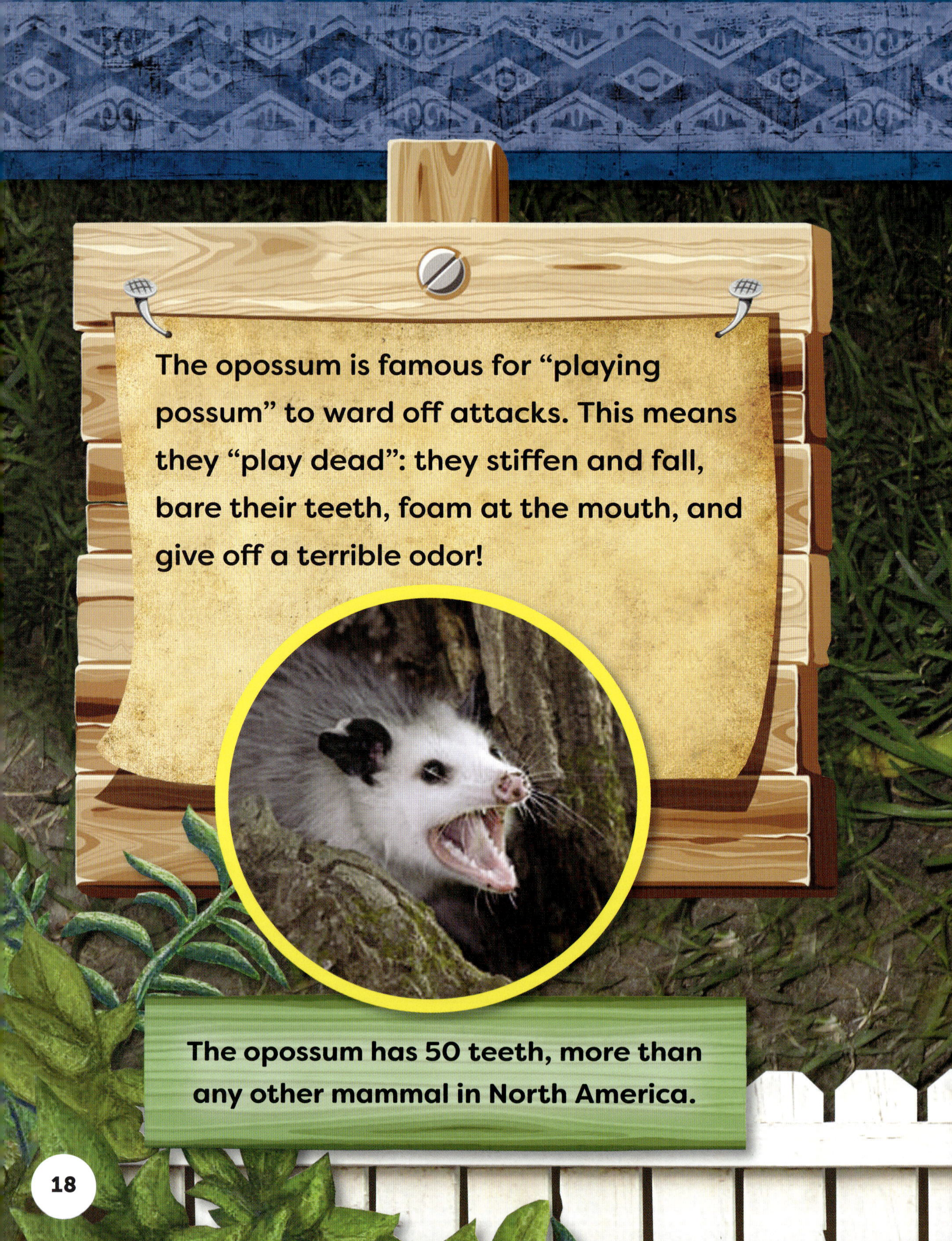

The opossum is famous for "playing possum" to ward off attacks. This means they "play dead": they stiffen and fall, bare their teeth, foam at the mouth, and give off a terrible odor!

The opossum has 50 teeth, more than any other mammal in North America.

We have interrupted the opossum's dinner. Opossums are known to eat almost anything, including seeds, nuts, fruits, worms, birds, eggs, snakes, insects, garbage, and dead animals!

After eating, the opossum uses its tongue to groom itself like a cat.

The opossum is the only marsupial in North America. That means the female has a pouch for carrying her young.

When the young are born after 13 days, they are no bigger than a honeybee!

Right after birth, the tiny babies crawl into their mother's pouch and attach themselves to one of her teats. Mama has enough teats for 13 babies. They will stay in the pouch for two months, just drinking milk and growing.

When full-grown, an opossum is the size of a house cat and can weigh 4 to 11 pounds (2 to 5 kilograms).

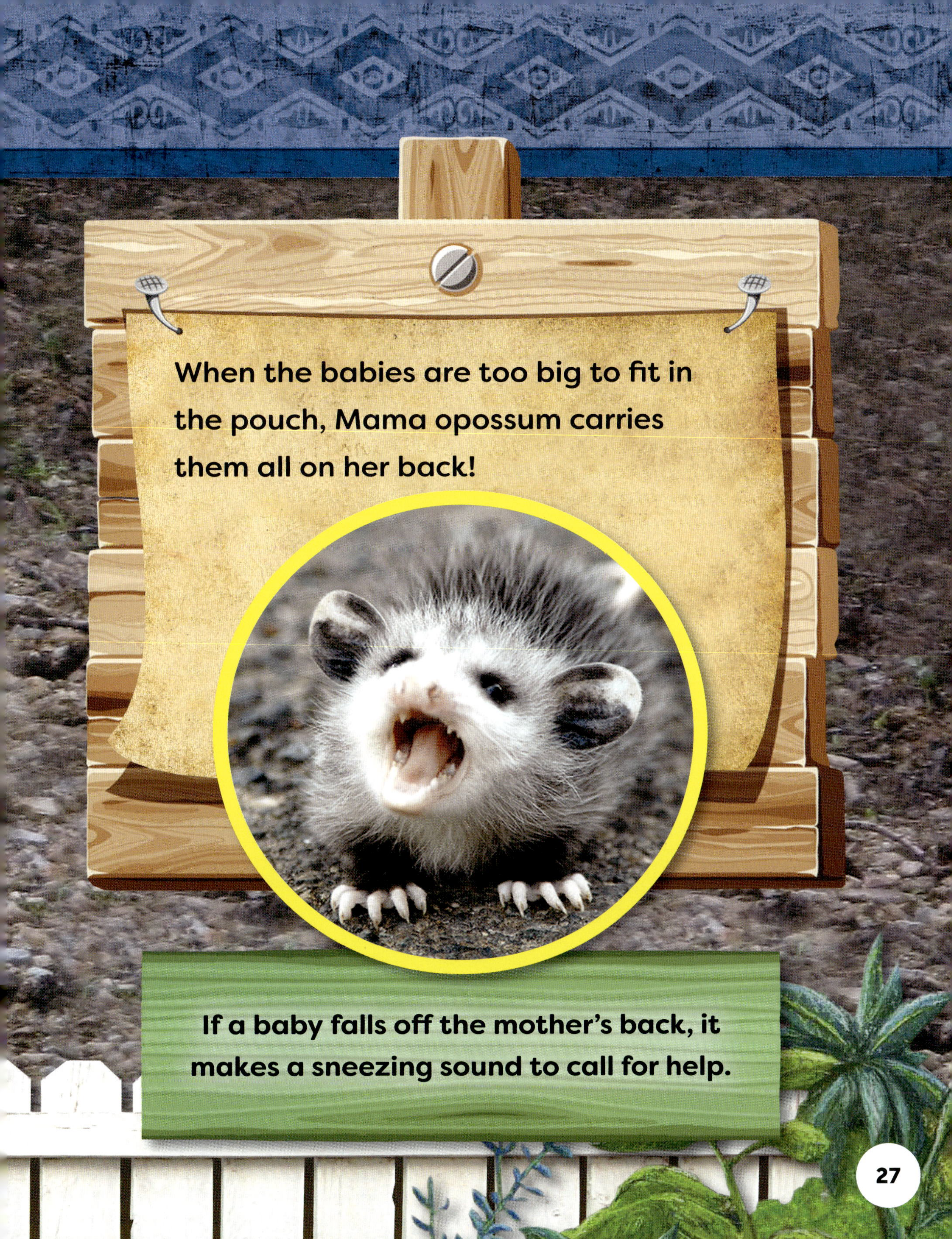

When the babies are too big to fit in the pouch, Mama opossum carries them all on her back!

If a baby falls off the mother's back, it makes a sneezing sound to call for help.

After four months, the babies will be big enough to leave their mother. Soon they will have babies of their own!

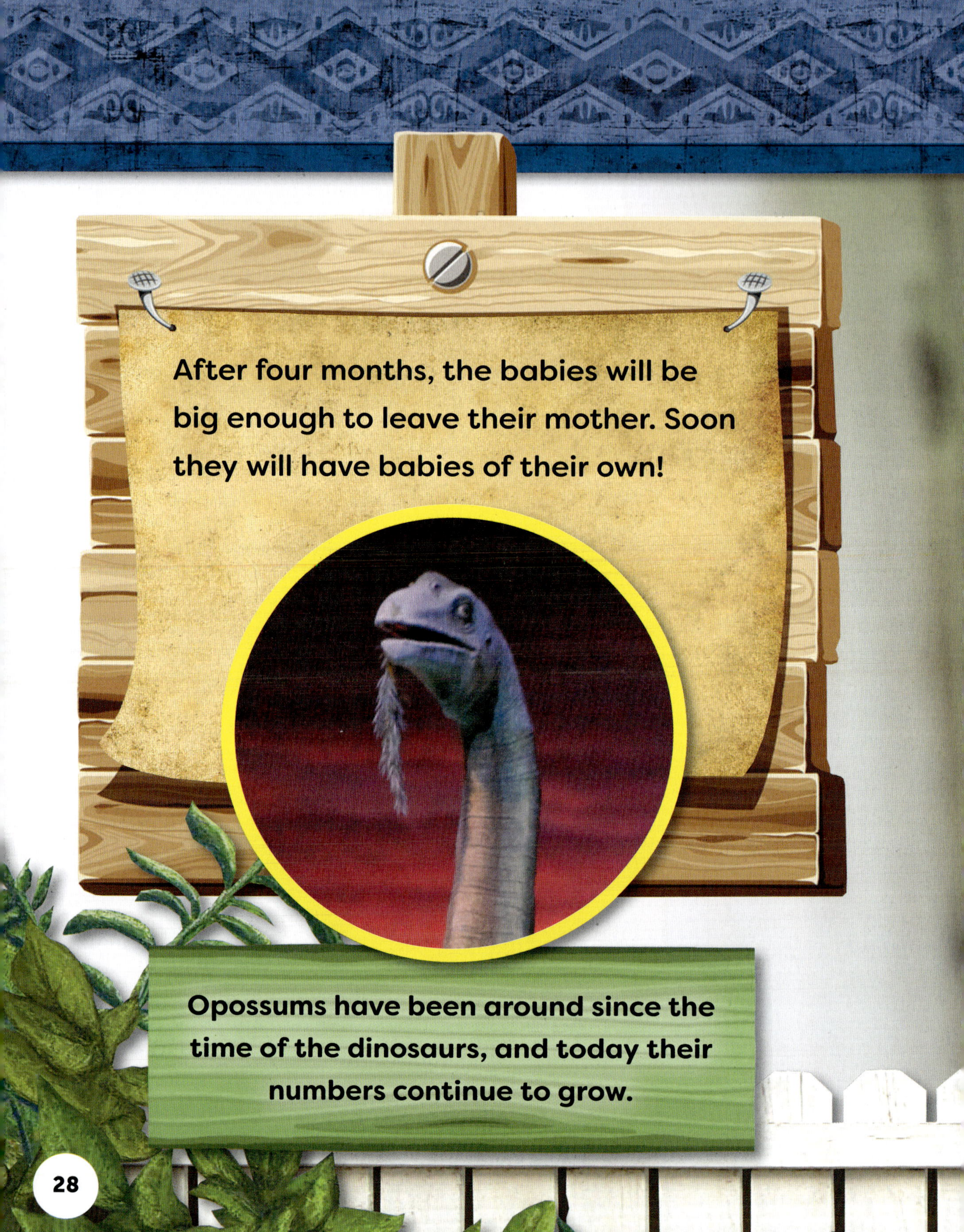

Opossums have been around since the time of the dinosaurs, and today their numbers continue to grow.

When the sun comes up, it will be time for the opossum to go to bed. Opossums sleep in tree holes or abandoned burrows made by other animals, like groundhogs and badgers.

Let's go back inside now so our friend can go on looking for dinner. Goodbye, opossum friend! Bon appétit!

FURTHER READING

Fictional Books Featuring Opossums

Bogue, Gary. *There's an Opossum in My Backyard*. Berkley, California: Heyday Books, 2007.

Walker, Sally M. *Opossum at Sycamore Road—A Smithsonian's Backyard Book*. Norwalk, Connecticut: Soundprint, an imprint of Palm Publishing LLC, 2011.

Fictional Books Featuring Opossums

Green, Emily K. *Opossums (Blastoff! Readers: Backyard Wildlife)*. Minneapolis, Minnesota: Bellwether Media, Inc., 2011.

Linde, Barbara M. *The Life Cycle of an Opossum*. New York: Gareth Stevens Publishing, 2011.

Whitehouse, Patricia. *Opossums (What's Awake?)*. Boston, Heinemann: A division of Houghton Mifflin Harcourt, 2009.

Works Consulted

Beer, Amy-Jane & Pat Morris. *Encyclopedia of North American Mammals,* San Diego: Thunder Bay Press, 2004.

Chinery, Michael, ed. *The Kingfisher Illustrated Encyclopedia of Animals*. New York: Kingfisher Books, 1992.

Reid, Fiona A. *Mammals of North American (Peterson Field Guides)*. New York: Houghton Mifflin Company, 2006.

Spelman, Lucy. *National Geographic Animal Encyclopedia*. Washington D.C.: National Geographic Society, 2012.

Wilson, Don E., & Sue Ruff, eds. *The Smithsonian Book of North American Mammals*. Washington & London: Smithsonian Institution Press, 1999.

On the Internet

National Possum Society
https://www.opossum.org/

INDEX